Women
and Their Children
Who Have
Survived Divorce

Janet Gosch

Cover photography: Richard R. Pixley & Lisa M. Vaughan
Layout and cover design: Sharp Graphic Design

Printed by   Sharp Printing Inc.
              3477 Lockport Road
              Sanborn, NY 14132

ISBN: 0-9679949-0-X

Library of Congress number: 00090777

"The world breaks everyone
and afterward many are
strong at the broken places."

Ernest Hemingway

For my husband, Bob Gosch,
who is my soul mate
and the epitome of a man;
and for my children, who are the best
God could have ever blessed me with.

Contents

Acknowledgments

In thanking people who have helped me with this book, I first must thank those who helped me through the darkest days of my divorce by sharing with me their time, advice, laughter and love; I could have never lived through those days without my faith in God and their support.

First and foremost, I want to thank my parents, Jack and Ann Westra, who were at my side every step of the way. They were there to help every time I needed it. They are the best!

I am indebted to my invaluable friends and advisors, Beth Ann Roberts, Robin Swedish, Lisa Almeter, Sue Rubins, Colleen Switala, Eileen Tutak and Carmelanne Caterisano.

I would like to thank from the bottom of my heart the women whose stories anonymously appear in this book. You've opened up your hearts to me so that others can learn and be inspired. I am so very grateful to each of you.

Introduction

I was divorced seven years ago; my life and the lives of my children seemed to change in an instant. Up to that point, the focus of my life was giving my two children, ages three and four, the best start possible in life. My life was my children; I never had much of a marriage.

Suddenly I was separated and feeling my life was out of control. One evening a week and every other weekend my children went off with my ex-husband and sometimes a girlfriend. They were confused; I was numb with pain. I had given everything I had to my children and I was now faced with so many unknown influences; the food they ate, the places they went, and the people they had contact with. Only a divorced mother can understand the pain -- it's devastating.

As mothers, we center our lives around our children for the most part. They depend on us for everything and we live to care for and protect them. We know the time will come when we will have to slowly let them spread their wings and fly from the nest. Never did I imagine that time would arrive when my children were so young. My four year old daughter looked at all of the changes that accompanied the divorce as a big adventure. My three year old son was scared and apprehensive. Within four months of my separation, I was working full time. My son went from being at home with me to being in day care all day. My daughter divided her time between day care and preschool. Every morning my son would be restrained at the day care window crying, "Mommy, mommy," with outstretched arms. I could do nothing but drive away. Each morning the guilt, anger and sadness I felt were overwhelming. The situation was out of my control. I could no longer do what was best for my children -- survival was now my main task. I thought I'd never smile again.

One evening, about nine months into my job as a single parent, I was lying on the couch crying -- overwhelmed with all that had to be done and feeling so sad that I could no longer give my children everything they needed and deserved. My daughter, then five, rubbed my arm and asked what was wrong. When I told her I didn't know if I could do it all, she said, "Mommy, you have to try like a gorilla, not a mouse." From the mouths of babes ...

It's seven years later and I have smiled again. My life is better than ever, but my relationship with my children has changed drastically and I struggle with the changes every day. But it is getting better.

The focus of this book is not my story but the struggle divorced mothers are up against. I feel recovery begins when you hear of someone who has experienced a similar situation and has overcome it. Divorced mothers need much more help and understanding than I saw was available to them. To read of positive outcomes from divorce can be very inspirational. I have compiled a collection of stories of women who have experienced life as single mothers with all of its trials, tribulations and triumphs so as to inspire other women experiencing divorce. They need to know there is light at the end of the tunnel.

My wish for all of you reading this: may you be inspired. For your sake and for the sake of your children, may you find inner peace, love and the strength to try like a gorilla.

Studies have proven that
despite the emotional difficulties
of living in a divorced family,
many children of divorce grow up
to be very responsible young adults.

Look back on your past
Don't stare ....
LEARN

Janet Gosch

Lucy

Lucy's children were four and six when she divorced in 1984. "Life does go on and eventually this does not consume your every thought." She has remarried "one of the most trustworthy men on the face of this earth" and he and her ex-husband get along. This has made the whole situation easier for everyone concerned.

My divorce took place mainly because of my husband's affairs. The first affair occurred while I was pregnant with my second son. We managed to make it through and then four years later, I walked in on him and another woman in my bed. That was the final straw.

Afterwards, I spent a lot of time blaming myself; if I would have just been thinner, spent more time with him, etc. etc. It takes a lot of time to get over blaming yourself.

My kids were 4 and 6 when we divorced. I think the most difficult part for me was that we moved away from my husband. My children cried every night asking for their daddy. They eventually adjusted to the new house, new school, our entire new life. I couldn't afford to keep the house we had owned, so this seemed like the best thing to do. In hindsight, it created too much disruption for the kids. Their entire world changed overnight, not to mention the emotional state of their mother.

Even though I have now married one of the most trustworthy men on the face of this earth, I still suffer from insecurity. I have recurring dreams that my husband has left me. I also seem to be extremely cautious and jealous. I try hard not to make my husband pay for my past, but it's so hard to just erase this from my being.

The children do not seem to show signs of continued emotional scars; however, I know that they have not had the secure life that they could have had if this had never occurred. I always envision what life would be like for my children had I not divorced. I constantly struggle with the guilt of not having provided them with a stable, secure home environment -- at least not to the standards that I feel they should have had.

I originally went to counseling at our church when my husband and I first separated; however, my husband was very concerned that the entire congregation would know about our problems. He was so concerned about this that I quit going to counseling. Neither I nor the kids ever sought any other help. To this day I believe that I would still benefit from going to counseling, even though I am now in a very secure and happy marriage.

My parents, especially Mom, provided me with constant security and support throughout the entire divorce. My mom is my ultimate source of security and strength. I also give credit to God. If I had not had my faith to cling to, I don't know what would have happened.

You do survive -- life will get better! Life does go on and eventually this does not consume your every thought. Every divorced person I know thinks at the time of divorce that he or she will never love again. I have never known anyone to actually not love again. It just takes awhile.

I have been divorced since 1984. I have been remarried to a wonderful man since 1987 -- a man who loves my kids as his own. My life now is much better than it ever was with my first husband. My ex-husband and I get along fine and communicate often about our boys. My ex-husband and my current husband even get along fine. This has made the whole divorce much easier to deal with. My children are now 19 and 17 and are becoming wonderful young men who do not appear on the surface to be scarred from the divorce. I still often wonder what impact it did have on them.

Janet Gosch

One hundred years from now,
it won't matter what car I drove,
what kind of house I lived in,
how much I had in my bank account,
nor what my clothes looked like; but
the world may be a little better because
I was important in the life of a child.

Anonymous

Janet Gosch

 Colleen

Married for 17 years with one son, she credits her son most for her survival. Colleen believes a mother must not let anyone ruin her life or the lives of her children. "My son gives me a reason every day to be happy. I'm not the one who has missed out."

My divorce occurred because my husband met a much younger woman and fell in love with her. He decided to tell me on New Year's Eve 1989 that he wasn't happy anymore. He said he wanted out and my whole world fell apart. We were married for 17 years and although we had a lot of ups and downs, I thought he was my partner for life. I wanted so much for our son to have a dad and a mom and a nice family life.

I am so lucky that my son adjusted to the divorce. He told me after my husband moved out how he used to lie in bed and listen to our fights. He told me how his heart would beat so fast and how he would wish we'd get a divorce. He was 11 years old at the time and a very smart child, but when all the fighting was going on, his grades were slipping. He was unhappy.

There are so many scars that will never heal. It was an abusive marriage at times, and my son may never forget the image of his mother being hit. Now he is 18 and is in college, but he still is bothered from time to time by the past. Although he tries to love his father, a lot of harm has been done. My son has a strong bond with me and credits me for keeping the roof over his head. The daily financial and emotional struggle is a scar that goes deep.

We never did get any outside help, but I did have a best friend who helped me through it all. She was very supportive and I talked to her a lot. My son and I tried to help each other but it's very easy to withdraw from everyone when the pain is very fresh. I felt like I would never get better; friends told me I would but I didn't believe them. I am very grateful to my son for the help he gave me. Children know and realize more than we think and deep inside they know when things are not right. My son gives me reason every day to be happy. I'm not the one who has missed out.

I give my son credit for my survival because after my husband left, I couldn't even function. I was lost. I couldn't cope and I was not able to help my son with his emotions. I would not get out of bed. One day my son came into my room when I was very upset. I told him I had nothing to live for. He said, "Mom, you have me to live for." I realized how selfish it was for me to say that. No person is worth the statement I made to my son. I love my son more than anything.

My husband's leaving has shown my son and me that we are stronger than we ever imagined. The lesson others could learn from my situation is that life goes on and one person should not be able to ruin your life and the lives of your children. When I look at my son, I am so proud of the way he has turned out. I do feel weak at times and I think single parenthood is the hardest job I've ever taken on. I always fear that I can't be strong enough to be the mom and the dad; but when I close my eyes to sleep at night, I do so knowing I've done the best that I could do for another day. My child will always know that I have stuck by him. We have a very close friendship.

I have been legally separated since 1989, but only divorced for one year. It took that long because no one wanted to pay for it and we didn't want anything material from each other. Life is not easy financially but emotionally we are stable. My son no longer lives in fear of his parents' fighting. It is a less stressful home environment without my husband. There is life after a failed marriage!

*Divorce is hard on adults,
but even tougher on kids.*

Janet Gosch

"A woman is like a tea bag:
you never know her strength
until you drop her in hot water."

Nancy Reagan

Janet Gosch

Rachael

Rachael got through it all by trying to keep focused, staying positive and praying.

My husband was transferred to the Buffalo area by his employer. I was to stay behind in Delaware, sell our house, take care of our two boys and all the other details that go along with relocating your family. We were delayed in moving to Buffalo and by the time we arrived, my husband had a girlfriend and a baby!

My children knew about the girlfriend because she had slept over when the children came to visit my husband in Buffalo. At first, my husband and his girlfriend told my two boys that the baby was her nephew. The children were devastated to learn the truth; the baby boy belonged to their father and his girlfriend. My boys were very mean to the little boy. He is now four years old.

My children say they will never get married. I think the hardest part is for them to forgive their father for lying to them about the baby. They do not want to visit him.

I was in therapy before I moved to Buffalo because of problems in the marriage before I even knew of the girlfriend. After the move, my children and I went to family counseling for one year. My children decided they didn't want to go anymore. Their father went only once with us.

I got through it all day by day. My pastor and friends at my church are very nice. I would have to say a male friend (not a boyfriend) was the strongest support I had. My girlfriends were also helpful taking me out for fun evenings. My family at first turned their backs on me because they all thought my husband was such a good person. Slowly, the truth surfaced.

I learned never to trust financial security to a man. I lost my house and am in debt $500,000 at this point because my husband was supposed to be making mortgage payments and paying bills from Buffalo while I was still living in Delaware. He maxed out all the credit lines and was quite deceitful while trying to cover two lives.

I have only been divorced for four months. I've just discovered my ex-husband borrowed $3,000 from my sister and her husband and he persuaded my mother to refinance her house and lend him $20,000. The money was borrowed while we were still married to supposedly help us out. I am now attempting to repay my family. What a mess!

I would love to meet a decent, honest man, but until I do, I try to keep focused, stay positive, and I pray. I have hope for my children and I try to be a good mother. It is very hard, but we'll get through it together. I hope to go back to school someday so I can leave this financial nightmare behind me.

We would never consider performing a tonsillectomy on a child without anesthetic, yet we do parent-ectomies on kids every day.

Janet Gosch

"Making the decision to have a child —
it's momentous.
It is to decide forever
to have your heart
go walking around
outside your body."

Elizabeth Stone

Janet Gosch

Mary is raising and loving her little boy all alone. She has learned from the past and hopes someday to find a good man who will work with her as a team.

The divorce occurred because my husband chose a lifestyle I could not live with. When we were first married, I had a good job. Shortly after the wedding, my husband quit his job. After four months of unemployment, he found a job. This lead to the pattern of my husband's working for a few weeks and then quitting. He then wanted me to take care of him while he partied with his friends every night. He would not return home many nights until dawn. When I suggested counseling, he would not cooperate. Finally he agreed to go for one session. He refused to go again. After we were evicted from where we were living and my husband was incarcerated, both for the second time, I chose to separate from him which eventually led to divorce.

We had one child together and the divorce has been extremely difficult for our son. It is hard for him to see other boys with their fathers. He asks a lot of questions about his father. I tell him about how his father and I did not get along. I just stuck with the marriage until I couldn't handle it anymore. I try to explain things in such a way that a three year old can understand.

I feel extremely bitter about the marriage and divorce. I think back about my marriage and feel I shouldn't have put up with all that nonsense for so long, but I did. If the roles were reversed my ex-husband would have walked away a lot quicker. I feel like I have been used. It is as if my son doesn't have a father because my ex-husband does not call or care to see the child. My son does not understand this. On a few occasions over the past summer my son has seen his father at the park where my ex-husband was playing horseshoes. My son would run up to his father and my ex-husband would ignore him. I could just see how hurt my little boy was. I am considering taking him to counseling to find out how to help him cope with his hurt.

The only help I have sought for us was talking to my mother and father. They were very supportive. My ex-husband could not be a good husband to me or a good father to my son. I am starting to talk to my son about everything and I'm encouraging him to ask questions.

I give myself credit for my survival. My idea of marriage was a husband and a wife living together in a home they bought together, working out problems and eventually raising a family. My ex-husband did not want to deal with any problems and he wanted to live like a single man. He usually thought of himself, but whenever he was in trouble, he expected me to be his safety net. I am glad I had the courage to get separated and divorced.

The most important lesson others could learn from me and my son is that you can get through it. I think about how our situation will get better. For me, my bitterness surfaces every day, but I don't let my son see any of it. I try to hug and kiss him every chance I get. I want the sadness in my son and the bitterness in me to decrease. I hope to someday remarry, but for now my son and I have each other. I tell him how much I love him every day.

I chose to stay home with my son during my separation. I did not want to put him in day care. Now that the divorce is final, he is in a Head Start Program and I am working in the evening. I want my son to know he can depend on me to take care of him, love him and provide for him. I feel sadness every day when I look at him and wish I could give him so much more. I can give him love, comfort and warmth, but I would like to give him a good life and future. I hope someday to find a man who will work with me as a team.

Janet Gosch

Children are more affected by the restructuring of the family and the way their feelings are handled more than by divorce.

This year mend a quarrel.
Seek out a forgotten friend.
Write a love letter.
Share some treasure.
Give a soft answer.
Encourage youth.
Keep a promise.
Find the time.
Forgive an enemy.
Listen.
Apologize if you were wrong.
Think first of someone else.
Be kind and gentle.
Laugh a little. Laugh a little more.
Express your gratitude.
Gladden the heart of a child.
Take pleasure in the beauty
and wonder of the earth.
Speak your love.
Speak it again.
Speak it still once again.

Anonymous

$\mathcal{L}ois$

Lois gives God and herself the credit for her survival. She proves to us there is life after two divorces!

My divorce was a result of my ex-husband's physical and mental abuse. He was emotionally distant, never home, and he was cheating with a woman he worked with. Before I knew of their relationship, he brought her to our home. He was an alcoholic. He stopped drinking for six years and then he began again. After ten years with him, I decided to reclaim my life.

My son never did get to spend a lot of time with his father, so he didn't suffer much throughout the divorce process. He is now realizing, however, that his father doesn't really care and is selfish. His father doesn't really bother with him, never calls, and only sees him once in awhile. My ex-husband doesn't buy him things either and my son sees the relationship other fathers have with their sons. I believe this hurts him more than the divorce. I do not feel my child will have any lingering emotional scars because he is very strong and we talk about everything. I also am strong, but less trusting of men and relationships.

This marriage I am discussing is my second. I have a 16 year old from my first marriage. I got both of my children very involved in friends, activities and church. We kept busy doing things together and we prayed a lot. This helped us get through it all.

I give God and myself the credit for my survival -- God for giving me the strength, intelligence, and ability to come to Him for guidance; myself for insight, courage and determination.

The most important lesson others could learn from what we have gone through is no one deserves to be abused; a relationship is not good if it hurts. To stay together for the children could end up hurting them more. There is life after divorce — a better life is waiting. You are lovable, you are strong and you are capable -- no man can strip a woman of these qualities no matter how hard he tries. You have only one short life -- happiness is yours if you believe in yourself.

I have been divorced for three years and life is much better. I can walk in peace without fear; I am closer to my kids. There is much less stress now. We all have a sense of belonging; before everything felt crippled like we were treading on eggs. Now we are living, not just existing. It is much harder financially, but money isn't everything -- peace of mind for myself and my children is most important.

My ex-husband remarried one day after our divorce was final -- to a woman he knew for about six months, someone much older than he. She takes care of him I guess. I am happy for him because they are so much alike. l feel bad; however, that it is so easy for men. He pays $47 a week in child support and his new wife supplies him with money. He drives a new car and he has no responsibilities -- it's all taken care of for him. As women, we struggle harder and are stronger for it. I believe this is why we are blessed with children. God knows we can handle it.

*It's smarter to send
your kids to college
rather than your lawyer's kids.*

Janet Gosch

THERE HAVE BEEN
ANGELS IN MY LIFE

There have been angels in my life.
While they haven't arrived with a blast
of trumpets or a rustle of wings,
I've known them just the same.
They performed their acts in human
guise, sometimes borrowing the faces
of family and friends, sometimes
posing as well-meaning strangers.
You have known them, too,
when just the right word was needed,
when a tiny act of kindness made a
great difference — or perhaps you
heard a voice whispering in the night
of sorrow, the words not quite clear
but the meaning unmistakable —
"There is hope — there is hope."

Anonymous

Janet Gosch

$\mathcal{L}$ori

Lori decided she could no longer stay in a dangerous situation. She was married to an alcoholic. Lori believes there is always hope for a better life.

My divorce occurred because my ex-husband, Chris is an alcoholic. He isolated himself from me and our daughters, Joyce and Brittany. There was mental and verbal abuse in our marriage. My self-esteem suffered because of this abuse and I began to have health problems because of the stress.

During the divorce, I took my children to a private psychologist. My oldest daughter, Joyce, is almost 13 years old, and she is able to see his true colors. My younger child, Brittany, is ten years old and she feels sorry for him. All of her anger is directed at me.

I was told by the psychologist my children are more cynical than other children their ages, but this may turn out to be a positive for them in their relationships in the future. As for myself, I have learned not to take abuse of any kind and as a result, I have my self-esteem back!

During the divorce process, a psychologist helped me and my daughters. My youngest daughter's school offers an in-school support group for children who are living through divorce. It is called the Banana Split group.

I give most of the credit for my survival to my wonderful family and a best friend who also went through a divorce. I recently became engaged and my fiance has been really understanding.

The most important lesson others could learn from what my children and I have gone through is if you're being hurt in any way and if all else fails -- never stay in a situation that is dangerous. There is always hope!

My divorce was final December 6, 1994 and my life has never been fuller or happier. My girls respect my fiance, but I think they are torn in some ways.

We are still having problems due to my ex-husband's alcoholism. He recently got a ticket for driving while intoxicated and there are many associated problems. He has a lot of anger and he uses the girls to get to me. I remain hopeful that things will work out.

Reassure children of all ages often that certain facts and feelings will never change; love between adults can change, but the love between parent and child Never ends.

Janet Gosch

JUST FOR TODAY

Just for today — I will live through the next 12 hours and not try to tackle all of life's problems at once.

Just for today — I will improve my mind. I will learn something useful. I will read something that requires thought and concentration.

Just for today — I will be agreeable. I will look my best, speak in a well-modulated voice, be courteous and considerate.

Just for today — I will not find fault with friend, relative or colleague. I will not try to change or improve anyone but myself.

Just for today — I will do a good turn and keep it a secret. If anyone finds out, it won't count.

Just for today — I will have a program. I might not follow it exactly, but I will have it. I will save myself from two enemies — hurry and indecision.

Just for today — I will do two things I don't want to do, just because I need the discipline.

Just for today — I will believe in myself. I will give my best to the world and feel confident that the world will give its best to me.

Anonymous

$\mathcal{L}$*inda*

Linda was able to overcome an abusive marriage, triumph over her past and become an attorney. She learned to believe in herself.

Why did the divorce occur?

Frank (who is a citizen of Lebanon, but a permanent resident) and I had been married for about three-and-a-half years. We had two beautiful children, Eric almost three years old, and Elizabeth, three months. I was supposed to return to work after my maternity leave, but instead decided to continue my education. I had an AAS in Paralegal and decided to go for my BA in Legal Studies because all the big law firms who paid well required a four year degree. Frank thought it was a great idea! He encouraged me in my studies, as long as I took out student loans to help out our budget.

After I was in school for about a month, Frank started getting upset with me quite frequently. He didn't like the amount of time I spent studying. He didn't like baby sitting the children on Tuesday nights when I had to take a three hour class. And he especially didn't like the fact that I had made some friends (female) at school, whom I studied with. He got mad one night and hit me across the face. Of course, he apologized and swore it wouldn't happen again. And it didn't — until the next week. Frank would get set off by the littlest things — like the dishes not being done immediately after dinner or if the laundry was done on a different day. He was upset if I was studying or doing homework, if the dinner wasn't hot enough, if I didn't pick up his clothes fast enough, or if he simply didn't like the way I looked. He started by hitting me across the face and then it progressed to beating me all over my body. He eventually broke my fingers, my hand and my jaw.

He was possessed! He was in control of my every move, and all of the money. I was convinced that I was at fault -- that I wasn't being a good wife, and that if I knew how to act properly, I would never get hit. He convinced me of this daily, constantly telling me how wrong I was, how stupid I was, and how terrible I looked. I put up with this for about two years. I learned how to cover the bruises. I learned to avoid people while things healed. I learned to tell stories of how I was injured.

Frank thought that I needed to be taught how to act like a proper wife, so he brought his mother to come stay with us for three months. She came over from Lebanon just before Christmas in 1991 and stayed until March 1992. This was the straw that broke the camel's back. She waited on him night and day; she would wake up at 5:00 a.m. to start cooking; and she cleaned constantly. I could see where he got his skewed views of what a wife should do. She was constantly criticizing me as well. I didn't do anything well enough. She begged Frank to leave me and come back home with the children to Lebanon. When I confronted Frank about this, he simply said he was considering it. I told him that I would never let him take the children there and he simply replied that it wasn't up to me; in fact, he would just kill me and take the children.

I knew I had to get out but I didn't know how. I had no self-esteem, no money, and no one to turn to. My family thought I should try to deal with my husband on my own. Besides, they had been unaware of the physical violence I had endured for the previous two years. I was in fear for my life and the lives of my children. I went to Immigration and told them what was happening and that I had been threatened. They sent me to the FBI. They were very helpful. We found out that Frank was trying to take out loans so that he could buy plane tickets for the children and himself. They told me I had to leave, so in March I did. My parents agreed to let me stay at their house for awhile -- I had FBI protection. My children's pictures were sent to the airports and borders, with instructions that they were not to be let out of the country. The FBI said that if he succeeded in getting them out of the country and into Lebanon, they wouldn't be able to help me at all. I got an order of protection and he had to stay away from me and my family. I had to pull my son out of the pre-school he attended. I had to take a leave of absence from school for a few weeks and literally had to stay under "house arrest" for my own protection.

A month later I was beginning to feel better about myself and felt powerful. I filed for divorce. After graduating from college in May of 1992, I was accepted into law school. I got my own apartment in a subsidized apartment complex. Since Frank was not paying any alimony or child support, I paid $8 a month rent. My divorce went through in August of 1992. I was 25 years old with a four-and-a-half year old son and two year old daughter.

How did the children cope and adjust throughout the divorce process?

My children knew that Daddy and Mommy fought; however, Frank tried to never let them see him hit me. But one time, just days before I left him, he beat me terribly in front of the children. Elizabeth was in her car seat in the back seat and didn't really pay that much attention; however, Eric was in the front seat and saw everything. Frank was angry because I was taking the children to visit my parents, so in order to stop me from going, he proceeded to beat my face into the hood of the car. I could see Eric screaming in the car, begging Frank to stop. When we left (for good) and I explained things to the children, Eric seemed relieved. He seemed to understand why we were at Grammy's house and why we weren't going to see Daddy for awhile. Elizabeth had a harder time. She had always been Daddy's little girl. She missed her father terribly. Although I had agreed to allow Frank to have supervised visitation, he decided not to. In fact from June until about November he didn't see the children at all.

The kids were excited about the new apartment and were making new friends. After awhile, Elizabeth stopped asking about Daddy. I think the children really liked the fact that Mommy seemed so happy all the time. And I was. Eric, however, was very protective of me (even for his young age). He clung to me, seeming to be a mama's boy for awhile. I remember the day that I came home and told them that Daddy and Mommy were divorced. I explained that we weren't married anymore, but that even though Daddy acted differently, Daddy still loved them very much and was a good father. I assured them the divorce had nothing to do with them and was not their fault. Elizabeth said she was sad; she cried. Eric just said it was okay and spent the rest of the day on my lap. Later that evening I talked about all of the good things that we were doing and were going to do; and how much fun it would be to just be the three of us. Because I was so up and so happy, the kids caught on. By the next day, everything was fine.

Do you or the children suffer from any emotional scars which you feel will never heal?

I think this is the hardest question to answer. My children seem to have adjusted quite well; although for about six months after the divorce Elizabeth would ask me when I was going to let Daddy come to live with us. With time, this stopped. Eric and Elizabeth are both doing very well in school, (Eric is in the gifted program), they have lots of friends, and they seem to be very well adjusted.

Frank has seemed to have come full circle. He sees the children every Wednesday night and has the children stay at his house every other weekend. They have a very good relationship with their father and with me. I don't know if they will have any scars in the long run. For now they show no signs.

As for me, I still feel sad about the divorce even though it was what I needed and wanted. I feel that the physical abuse I suffered will never be erased from my memory, nor should it be. I don't want to forget, for I don't want to ever go through that again (and won't). However, I feel that I have healed and will continue to heal. These emotional scars don't affect me in any negative way now, but it has taken me a long time to get here.

What help, if any, did you get for yourself and/or the children?

I had a psychologist do a brief interview with both children to determine if they would need any help — she thought that they were both doing very well in light of the circumstances and thought that they were adjusting normally; therefore I did not seek any further help for them.

As for myself, I did seek some counseling for about three months after my divorce as I was suffering from severely low self-esteem and was feeling quite worthless. I later learned that this is a common side effect of an abusive relationship.

The counseling helped me gain back much of my self-esteem and I looked at myself in a whole new light. I knew my life was now in my own hands (along with my children's) and I was the only one to make decisions and be in charge of my life. It did help tremendously!

To what or whom do you give the most credit for your survival?

The most credit for my survival has to go to me. The counseling helped me to feel good about myself and sent me in the right direction, but, ultimately I had to rely on myself. You have to rely only on yourself -- that's the biggest thing you learn going through this. Friends and family members can be there to offer support and a shoulder to lean on, but they can't push you through the day to day stuff; only you can do this. And I believe this is how it should be. We can't rely on others to make us happy and have productive, full, wonderful lives. We must do this on our own. The sooner one realizes this, the sooner one will be able to make it through.

What is the most important lesson others could learn from what you and your children have gone through?

I think the most important lesson is believing in yourself, knowing that you are a capable, intelligent human being who can live your own life and make your own decisions. You are responsible for the lives of your children as well. Also remember that the road of divorce is a hard and winding one to travel, with many potholes and dangerous curves along the way, but with clear thinking and a plan or map of where you want to go, you will get there with few or no casualties.

Another extremely important lesson is to keep the best interest of your children in mind. It is extremely hard for children to go through a divorce -- we have to acknowledge this first. Then we must also think about what it is like to completely lose a parent. Especially if we have sole custody, we must remember that although we can no longer tolerate and live with a spouse, that spouse is still a parent of our children. Try not to make the other parent seem "bad" in the children's eyes; try not to speak badly about the other parent or slant your children's perspective. They need that other parent unless, of course, the other parent presented a threat or danger to your children. They should be able to benefit from both a mother and father -- even if they aren't all living in the same house. This is one of the hardest things to do, but it must be done for the sake of the children.

Also, we should be aware of our emotional and physical needs throughout the divorce process. Obviously any physical needs should be met first, but also pay attention to your mental state and that of your children. There is no shame in getting help -- in fact that's the first step in recovery -- admitting that you do need help. Whether it's counseling or talking with a friend or whatever, get it and use it so that you can be on your way to being self-sufficient and living your own life again.

How many years have you been divorced and what is life like now for you and your children?

I have been divorced for about four and one half years now. Life right now is pretty good for both me and the children. After the divorce I put myself through law school. I graduated and have a pretty good job. I really like who I am and where I am in my life. I live in a really nice duplex in a great neighborhood. My children are doing well in school and have lots of friends. They have continued adjusting and have a great relationship with their father. I haven't had any problems with either of them and don't really anticipate having any.

Any additional comments?

The hardest thing for me right now is dating. After going through the "all men are scum" stage after the divorce, I realized all men aren't scum and there are some pretty nice guys out there. Just recently though I have really thought about wanting to be married again. I do want to get married again. I am a totally different person now than I was a few years ago and I want to share my life with a man who can appreciate who I am. That's hard. I'll be 30 next month and I have a 9 year old boy and a 6 year old girl; this scares a lot of men. I've met quite a few who aren't ready for a "package deal." I am also very self-confident, outgoing, intelligent, attractive, self-sufficient -- traits which scare the rest of the men. They have a hard time dealing with a woman attorney who knows what she wants from life. Most of them can't handle my self confidence, my self sufficiency, and my independent thinking. But I am optimistic that Mr. Right is still out there somewhere -- I just have to find him.

Janet Gosch

*Anger is only
disappointed hope.*

Janet Gosch

"You don't get to choose
how you're going to die or when.
You can only decide
how you're going to live."

Joan Baez

$\mathcal{L}isa$

Lisa found the Welfare to Work Program invaluable. Her young son was diagnosed with leukemia during the divorce process. Today he is in remission and Lisa is an optician.

My ex-husband and I were very different people. We were married for six and a half years. He was extremely controlling. He brought me down; he made me feel worthless. He felt because I was not bringing any money into the marriage my opinion did not matter. He made me feel like I needed to depend on him for everything. Our ideas for the future and our morals and values were completely opposite. I was in and out of counseling. I wanted to try to make my marriage work. Finally, I realized I had to leave, for things were not going to change.

When I was going through the divorce, my sons were nine months and five years old.

Three months into the divorce process, my older son was diagnosed with leukemia. I never thought I could handle the stress and strain of it all. My ex-husband's pride got in the way because I left him; therefore, he was not supportive through my son's illness. I had no money and no choice but to go on Welfare. Seven years later, my son is in remission. I don't think of the possibility of the cancer reoccurring because I couldn't function. He thinks he is invincible. He has survived his parents' divorce, cancer and repeating Kindergarten which was a very traumatic experience for him, but he and I are still angry. We both have been in counseling for four years.

My youngest son is unaffected because he doesn't ever remember his father living with us .

I could have never survived the entire situation without the Welfare to Work Program. Without this program I could have never afforded to go back to school and take care of my sick son at the same time.

I also received a lot of help from my family and friends; my parents watch my children a lot. I very much wanted to prove to my ex-husband I could do it alone and I have. I found a lot of inner strength. I am the first in my family to graduate from college. I am now an optician and I love my job.

The most important lesson others could learn from what my children and I have gone through is a person is never stuck in a situation. I found so much help was available through the Welfare Program and Housing and Urban Development (HUD) assistance. My children and I are stronger than ever.

I am tired of being alone. I live my life for my children and I work full-time. I am very intolerant of men because of what I've been through, but I don't want to be lonely forever.

I have been divorced for seven years. Life is a struggle but it is better. I receive $100.00 a week from my ex-husband in child support. He destroyed our lives for a while, but not forever. It is very difficult to have a life of my own when I'm so busy working and taking care of my kids. My ex-husband only sees the children when it's convenient for him. He is remarried and has two more children and one child from a previous marriage. I hope someday to find a man to share my life with. I want my sons to know how a good man and a good father lives his life.

ediation

Growing in popularity but not appropriate for everyone, mediators help a divorcing or an already divorced couple define their issues and reach an agreement. Mediators work on reorganizing the family into two separate units; this idea is extremely comforting to children. The mediator's goal is to get to the issues that lie buried under the anger and resentment felt by the parents. This service is almost always less expensive than legal fees and it encourages parents to look to the future.

For more information:

Academy of Family Mediators
5 Militia Dr.
Lexington, MA 02421
(781) 674-2663

Divorces don't ruin children's lives, people do.

"Life is either a daring adventure
or nothing at all."

Helen Keller

Janet Gosch

 Beverly

Divorced 32 years ago, Beverly says, "I have never had the desire to remarry and I know I never will because I love my life."

My divorce occurred because my ex-husband and I were too young to take on the responsibility of marriage and he was running around with other women. At the time of my divorce my children were four, six and eight years old. They were my first concern, so I was very careful who I dated. The most difficult time for me was my children's teen years. They were difficult to handle. My youngest had a lot of problems in school. I had to keep a close watch on him.

I don't think we've suffered any emotional scars. I got a lot of help from my parents and my sisters. They watched my children and picked them up from school when they were sick. I also had a neighbor who my children stayed with after school until I got home.

Unfortunately my ex-husband wasn't much help. He would pick them up when it was convenient for him. He never kept them overnight and rarely did he feed them meals.

I give the most credit to myself for my survival. A single mother needs to feel positive about a situation. I coped because I always felt there was someone in a worse situation. I thank God my children and I are healthy.

The most important lesson to be learned from my situation is this: a single mother feels sorry for her children in a divorce so she tries to make up for it by giving in to them, spoiling them, buying them everything they ask for or even letting them do things or go places they should not. She must learn to say no and stick to it. Children can wear you out but you must stay strong and do what it best for them. And, of course, love them and don't be afraid to tell them. I remember my son once saying to me, "I'm going to live with dad." I told him he couldn't because I love him and would miss him too much.

I have been free for 32 years. I was divorced in 1967. Two of my children are married and one is divorced. I have five grandchildren. I see my ex-husband at family gatherings with his third wife and we all get along fine. I like his current wife because of the way she treats my children.

My children told me I did a good job raising them. I have good children. They have never gotten into trouble and are hardworking.

I was married for ten years and quit working as soon as my daughter was born. I never had the desire to work when my children were young, but when I divorced I had to go back to work and I also returned to school for my Bachelor's Degree. Eventually I received my Master's Degree in Education.

I have had great relationships with men through the years, but my family still comes first. I enjoy visiting with them and have a great time with my grandchildren. I have never had the desire to remarry and I know I never will because I love my life.

AFTER A WHILE

After a while you learn the subtle
difference between holding a hand and
chaining a soul and you learn that love
doesn't mean leaning and company
doesn't always mean security.
And you begin to learn that kisses aren't
contracts and presents aren't promises
and you begin to accept your defeats
with your head up and your eyes ahead
with the grace of a woman and not the
grief of a child.
And you learn to build all your roads
on today because tomorrow's ground
is too uncertain, for plans and futures
have a way of falling down in mid-flight.
After a while you learn that even sunshine
burns if you get too much so you plant
your own garden and decorate your own
soul instead of waiting for someone
to bring you flowers.
And you learn that you really can endure,
that you really are strong and you really
do have worth and you learn and you
learn, with every goodbye you learn.

Veronica A. Shoffstall

Janet Gosch

 Dorothy

Dorothy raised eight children. She encourages others to be open to help at the first sign of problems.

My ex-husband was affected by his childhood. When we married, he never trusted me or would believe anything I told him. As we had children, he could not adjust or handle the financial and emotional responsibility of a family. After counseling I was told he was a paranoid schizophrenic with homicidal tendencies. He was both physically and mentally abusive to my children and me.

After the divorce my children went through a very bad period. My youngest children were twins. They were held back in first grade. Another child had problems in school right through high school and is still the most insecure of my eight children.

I don't think any one of my children ever adjusted at all. They were used by my ex-husband to threaten me with court procedures. If they needed things I could not afford, he would say he could take them and all would be wonderful. My children felt as if they were always causing me problems and their feelings became a handicap for me to deal with. My children and I all suffer from emotional scars which we feel will never heal. Most of my children have become estranged from their father and some have minimal contact with him.

I have remarried and often I will become angry or defensive because I have flashbacks whenever I am in a situation that I can identify with from my past.

I don't know if I can truly ever become close to my new husband, because if he shows me any sign of floundering I become panicky and feel he will become the maniac I divorced.

I felt that it was a stigma to go to counseling, but I did go for the children which eventually brought the whole family into counseling. It was enlightening and semi-helpful. I went to Tough Love for my most troubled child. Unfortunately I, myself, was in limbo for far too many years and was too late getting the right direction or answers.

I give the most credit for my survival to LINK, a support group operated through the Catholic Church. I am still close with my original LINK group. It was a Godsend to me, and the support and camaraderie that we have is to be cherished. I thank God for guiding me in that direction.

When I divorced I lived in the suburbs and most all of my family and friends were ten to 15 miles away. I didn't have a lot of friends then, but when I went back to work and rejoined the human race, I slowly became the person I was when I was younger.

The most important lesson others can learn from what I and my children have gone through is at the first sign of problems or trouble in your marriage seek help with your mate. If he won't go, go alone. Don't waste years trying to work out hopeless situations and put the children through needless stress, abuse and anxiety.

Move on and don't feel your life is over. Don't think you are alone. Don't be embarrassed. These feelings make you try to keep your terrible life a secret and only compound your problem. Be open to family and friends. Release your problems to the fresh air and the light of reality. It will move you forward.

I have been divorced for 12 years and I remarried one and a half years ago. I felt like a child bride at my wedding and everyone marveled at how happy I looked and the glow on my face. That was because I opened my heart and life to another, and I have such confidence that we will succeed. Many of my children attended my wedding. They came from California, Georgia, Texas and New York. My youngest child left for Egypt the day before my wedding. He cried when he watched the video. He was heartsick because he couldn't be with us. We're very close.

I cherish my children and the bond we have came from the tragedy we suffered. Unfortunately, my ex-husband forfeited 95% of his family life and ties with his actions. Now I can say it was worth the effort with my children, but I do wish I had had more knowledge to accomplish what I did accomplish raising them alone.

There are no guarantees in life or in marriage, but doing something is better than doing nothing. It is so rewarding to advance instead of being locked in terror. I have given advice to so many and find it great to observe the progress of those I have helped.

Children don't believe in no-fault divorce. They blame one or both parents or themselves.

"Far away there in the sunshine
are my highest aspirations.
I may not reach them but I can look up
and see their beauty,
believe in them and try to follow them."

Louisa May Alcott

Janet Gosch

Margaret

"Have goals in your life and keep religion in your life."

My divorce occurred because my ex-husband claimed that he was unhappy. He said I wasn't what he wanted me to be. My ex had a heart attack at 36 years old, just ten months prior to me being served with divorce papers. I helped and supported him back to a healthy person. He went back to work and served me shortly after. There supposedly was not another woman involved, but his late nights always put question in my mind. I have learned not to dwell on the reason.

My three children have been in turmoil since the day I got served in October, 1994. Even though we have grown, the frustration in their lives is still there. My oldest child has had to face things that she definitely is not ready for. If I cried, they cried. In the process of the legal battle, my three children had become bargaining chips for him to use. My ex-husband used them to get at me. As I became to realize what our marriage was all about, the control he had over me lessened.

I will always have a small emotional scar as will my three children. My oldest child is my biggest worry. She has seen my ex hurt me emotionally and physically and has very little hope or faith in man/woman relationships.

I went to counseling through Catholic Charities immediately after being served with divorce papers. I realized

I needed help in sorting out what I was and what I wanted to be. I immediately advised my children's teachers as to the situation and did get them involved in any support groups that were available.

I give the most credit for my survival to myself and my family. I have a mother and four brothers I couldn't have made it without. My dad has been in a Veterans' Hospital since I have been little so I basically grew up without him. My four brothers are all married and they are wonderful fathers and husbands. Along with them and my sisters-in-law, I had a fantastic support system whenever I needed it. They were always there to help me with my children. My mom tried to help me financially whenever she could -- just baby sitting my children so I could work helped. My brothers took my kids overnight and helped my children to always realize that there are good fathers out there.

The most important lesson others could learn from what I and my children have gone through is to be aware of what is going on around you. Work at a marriage every day. Don't lose yourself. Be independent. Don't expect someone else to do everything for you. Have goals in your life and keep religion in your life.

I have been legally divorced since January 1996. My life is somewhat hectic. My three children, all girls, ages six, seven and thirteen, keep me going. I have returned to college full time. I work thirty hours a week, keep up a home and try to have some fun socially. I joined a support group and now I am training to be a facilitator.

I became friends with a man from my support group and fell into a relationship that lasted only four months. I did experience something that I hadn't had in my life in a long time and I truly believe God put that man in my life so my bitterness and anger over my ex-husband would disappear and it did.

I went back to college right after my ex-husband left. I always wanted to finish college and I never did. I have learned a lot about people, gained some wonderful friendships, lost 50 pounds, regained my self-esteem and learned about controlling the things I can and letting go of the things I cannot control.

I have become a new person -- or I should say I found part of the old me that was lost in my marriage. I have faced the blame and the failure of my part of our marriage. I realize and have accepted that we were two different people. I was willing to work at our marriage and my ex-husband was not. You cannot control other people's actions.

So, now I can only be the best that I can and even though I have times that I fall down, I can only get up and try again. I have no one in my life right now and sometimes I get down about wishing someone would come into my life to share a date once in a while. Obviously it's just not meant to be -- now.

Even though my ex doesn't take the kids when he is supposed to, I learned not to worry any more. It is a loss to him. He moved in with a woman and lives two blocks from my home. My ex-husband and his girlfriend fight constantly. It is not good for the children.

I am completely over him and I think sorting everything out in small steps has helped. We are back in court for financial reasons. He hasn't paid me what we agreed to in legal contract. He uses the children all the time, as he thinks that by not taking them punishes me. I am able to not let this frustrate me any longer. It is definitely his loss.

Janet Gosch

Serenity Prayer

Grant me the serenity
to accept the things I cannot change,
the courage to change the things I can,
and the wisdom to know the difference.

Janet Gosch

"Love yourself first
and everything else falls into line.
You really have to love yourself
to get anything done in this world."
Lucille Ball

Janet Gosch

"The lesson learned is that mistakes and/or failures can lead to new opportunities and success."

My spouse of eleven years became very withdrawn and requested a separation. A year later a divorce was granted. Our relationship did not have trust as a basis. This foundation was missing and it was only a matter of time that the marriage would dissolve. My marriage lasted as long as it did because I conceded a great deal. In the end, even that didn't help.

My children appeared to adjust, but as I look back and still see today, they did not adjust very well and, in fact, neither did I. My daughter clung to me during her early childhood and feared I would leave her too. She did express her fears which was good. My son was silent and did have problems in school and was expelled in his tenth grade year. Counseling proved futile.

After my divorce I went to a psychologist to repair or help me cope with my feelings of rejection, loss of self-esteem and feelings of failure. I wanted to explore my own weaknesses and responsibility in the failed marriage. The counseling helped immensely. As we went down the road of my childhood, I was not prepared for the revelations that were surfacing. I was supported also by friends who helped restore my self-worth. I went to work and renewed my ability to see myself as a survivor and not a victim. I read every book I could get my hands on -- anything that would help explain my current situation.

I do feel my children and I will always suffer from some emotional scarring. I still have dreams I'm married to my first husband. When I first remarried, I would assume the worst from my second husband's behaviors and found myself still reacting to my first husband's negative behaviors. My son, now 31, continues to be single and continues to display some anti-establishment behaviors. My daughter married a man very similar to her father.

The most important lesson others could learn from what I and my children have gone through is I have been very supportive of marriage and the rewards of it. As I remarried, I was vigilant in assessing problem areas. My husband and I took part in Marriage Encounter and we worked at communication.

Another lesson learned is that mistakes and/or failures can lead to new opportunities and success. The emotional lows end and you can be happy in a loving, healthy relationship. You have to like yourself and respect yourself first.

I have been divorced for 20 years. My children live on their own. I am in a very happy, stable marriage and my children have come to love and respect their stepfather. My son probably will never marry and my daughter is going through divorce proceedings. Thankfully, she does not have children. My daughter is upset and is examining her own choices.

I think there should be groups established for young people about to enter marriage or shortly after marriage to help them with tools for communication and to learn from each other.

Communication in marriage is so very, very important.

ONE DAY AT A TIME

There are two days in every week about which we should not worry, two days which should be kept free from fear and apprehension.

One of those days is YESTERDAY, with its mistakes and cares, its faults and blunders, its aches and pains. YESTERDAY has passed forever beyond our control.

All the money in the world cannot bring back YESTERDAY. We cannot undo a single act we performed; we cannot erase a single word we said, YESTERDAY is gone.

The other day we should not worry about is TOMORROW, with its possible adversaries, its burdens, its large promise and poor performance. TOMORROW is beyond our immediate control.

TOMORROW'S sun will rise, either in splendor or behind a mask of clouds — but it will rise. Until it does, we have no stake in TOMORROW, for it is as yet unborn.

This leaves only one day - TODAY. Any man can fight the battles of just one day. It is only when you and I add the burdens of those two awful eternities — YESTERDAY and TOMORROW — that we break down. It is not the experiences of TODAY that drive men — it is the remorse or bitterness for something which happened YESTERDAY and the dread of what TOMORROW will bring.

Let us, therefore, live but ONE DAY AT A TIME.

Janet Gosch

Debbie

The divorce occurred because my ex-husband and myself outgrew each other. My ex-husband had gotten into using drugs. All he wanted to do was smoke pot and sleep. It was hard to get him to work. He only worked when he had to. My life had become a disappointment and my children were taking the brunt of it all.

My ex-husband had become even more abusive than when we first met. There were outbreaks of throwing dishes and furniture and him beating me. I knew that I couldn't live like that any more and I didn't want my children to be subjected to that either. It wasn't easy walking on eggshells, afraid I'd say the wrong thing. After he put me in the hospital I felt so stupid and ashamed; I finally got a divorce, knowing that if he came after me again he might kill me.

My children were very confused throughout the divorce process. I couldn't spend the time most mothers do with their children. I was working and worrying and crying a lot and the kids -- Paul age five, and Susan age three, picked up on this. Their father never picked them up and the children felt very rejected. He refused to pay child support and everyone, especially the kids, suffered. The three of us became very close to each other.

It is still hard for me to trust people, especially men. I have never stopped working since I got divorced. I need to know I can take care of myself. I try not to depend on anyone but me.

My daughter Susan committed suicide at the age of 16. I guess that speaks for itself. That was eight years ago. I blamed the divorce on this situation, this tragic situation.

My son, Paul, is far too serious about life. It is very hard for him to have fun. He judges himself too harshly and tries to be a perfect father. He is now 26 years old and married. He tries to be perfect in everything he does. He has a hidden anger. He's trying now to build some sort of relationship with his father.

We sought counseling at Catholic Charities when we were going through the divorce. We went for about a year. I had to get food stamps and aid for babysitting. With all the help there is a person can never put Humpty Dumpty back together again. All you can do is pick up the pieces and go on with your life.

I owe my survival to my mother and my family. My religion and faith in the Lord pulled me through all of my hardships. My family was always there for me. I had also met a friend who I could talk to and share some of my burdens with. I talked a lot with the priest at our church and he helped me to get an annulment.

The most important lesson others can learn from what we've gone through is you can never change a person no matter how much you love them. When you're young you really think that will happen but it doesn't. Sometimes the person gets worse instead of better. Listen to what others say. This can be important because they see with clear vision where you just see with love.

Develop self-esteem in children at a young age so that they can evaluate people better when they get older. Also, help them to have confidence in themselves so that the world isn't so scary a place.

I have now been divorced for 20 years. I have been remarried for 17 years. I was lucky to meet someone who loved me and cared for me and treated me like a lady.

When a woman remarries you bring all the baggage with you from your first marriage. It takes twice the work to keep it together the second time.

I really feel that the children never really overcome the trauma of the divorce. It scars them for life.

I was blessed to have a third child with my second husband. She is a diamond. All my children were blessings, but this one has been raised by a mom and a dad who have always been there for her.

The confusion that the divorce caused in feelings and loyalty to a parent was something my third child never had to deal with. At this point she appears to be very well-adjusted and she always feels very much loved.

"When God closes a door,
he always opens a window."

Janet Gosch

Janet Gosch

My ex-husband and I met when I was 21 years old and looking for a way out of my hometown. He lived in Illinois and I lived in New York at the time of our meeting. We carried on a long distance romance and were together approximately 35 days before we married one year after we met. I remember walking down the aisle thinking that I don't even know this person.

We were married for ten years. I don't believe my ex-husband was ever completely committed to our marriage. I truly never had a clue as to what was happening. I was so young and naive and I was living far away from my family. I knew he was extremely secretive and private and I knew I was so very lonely in my marriage, but I tried to make the best of it. We moved back to my hometown with our two little children and that's when I found out my ten year marriage had been basically a sham. I felt like everyone in the world knew except me.

When we separated, my children were ages three and four. It is so painful to even think back on those times. I went back to teaching full time three months after we separated. The kids' world was turned upside down. Overnight they went from having a totally devoted, loving mother who worked part time in the evenings to a crazed, angry mother who was either at work or emotionally unavailable.

The more I found out about my ex-husband's life outside our marriage — I was at times unable to function. The problem was I had to go to work every morning and come home to two very needy little children.

In situations like this, which is unfortunately becoming much too common, ex-husbands like to tell their girlfriends that their ex-wife is crazy — and they're right. I was crazy. I was crazy trying to deal with the knowledge that my husband who was supposed to be my partner and helpmate had chosen to throw away the family for his own desires.

I was crazy because I had to now not only take care of the children physically and mentally but also take care of the house, the bills, the car, the yard, the wash, my job, meals and my physical and mental health. I had to deal with girlfriends who wanted to play mom to my little children and last, but not least, I was crazy because suddenly I was back in the dating game. I left my first date in tears. I felt like such a fool on a date again after ten years of marriage.

So through all of this craziness the ex-wife is supposed to remain sane. It's an overwhelming, exhausting task.

Another important point to make is when my ex-husband picked up the kids one evening a week and every other weekend, he was rested and ready to have fun. I was heartbroken that I had to send my kids out the door with their car seats and my baby son with his diaper bag. I usually would not hear from them until they returned home two days later. I missed and worried about them so much.

I will never forget one of the first girlfriends my ex-husband introduced the kids to. Marie tried so very hard to get the kids to like her. Soon after my children met Marie I took the kids to a bike path near our home. I was sitting on a bench so exhausted and depressed I could barely move. My daughter, who had recently turned five, rode her bike up to me and said, "Mommy, Marie is so fun. Yesterday she baked brownies for us, bought us bubbles, painted my nails and let me try on all of her jewelry. She's so fun. I wish she was my mommy." I now believe a broken heart is a true physical condition because at that moment I felt my heart break.

Our lives turned into an emotional roller coaster ride. I struggled every day to survive to make a good life for my kids, but every day my kids were confused and torn. I had lots of rules and boundaries for my kids. With my ex-husband life was much more fun.

My ex-husband would drop off the kids on a Sunday evening and sometimes my daughter would literally pass out on her bed from exhaustion. My son would squirm around on the floor and not want to talk. I got to know many counselors and many therapists. I just wanted my children to have a normal childhood.

Every single day was a challenge. I could have never survived without my faith in God. I just believed in my heart things would someday get better. I truly believed that when God closes a door, he opens a window.

My parents were always there for me. They would do anything for me. My mother listened to me better than anyone else. I also could not have survived without my incredible friends, my beautiful children, the many hours of counseling I received, support groups and, most of all, my best friend, Bob. Bob is that window God sent to me when he closed the door.

Divorce is a process my friend, Jill, once told me and it's true. My children and I have come so far since 1992, but it will never be completely behind us. During the divorce, my daughter turned to food for comfort, but is now moving towards healthier habits. She is very determined, intelligent and beautiful. I'm sure she'll succeed in every goal she sets for herself.

My son was labeled dyslexic but he has overcome his previous lack of confidence. My son's teachers say he could not work harder than he does or have a better attitude. He's a darling, smiling boy with a very loving, sensitive heart.

I still have not finished this whole healing process. I feel the last step for me is to totally forgive my ex-husband. I know I won't be completely free until I reach that point of forgiveness, but I'm still trying to figure out how to get there.

I owe it to myself and my family to never give up on the process.

The most important lesson others could learn from what we have gone through is don't turn a blind eye to troubles in your relationship.

I was never able to communicate on the level I needed to with my ex-husband. This always bothered me. You can't change a person. Know the person you choose to marry inside and out. Know their family, know their past, know their hopes and dreams for the future and know yourself before you marry. Marriage with children needs to be a lifelong commitment from both parties involved. Divorce is too traumatic for adults; how are children supposed to deal with it?

My life now seven years after my separation and divorce is like a dream come true. Four and a half years ago I married my soulmate, Bob. Eleven months later I gave birth to a beautiful, healthy baby. Because of Bob's unfaltering love and support, I've been able to put this book together so others may be helped, supported and possibly inspire to move ahead with hope.

There was many a moment back in 1992 when I felt I could never survive. What was to become of me and my two little children? I felt like I was in a cold, lonely, dark hole. It was then I realized a simple fact of life. When you find yourself in a hole where life has fallen in on top of you, there are two choices: (a) stay in the hole, or (b) pull yourself out. There will be others there to assist you, but you ultimately have to do most of the pulling and climbing by yourself.

In the inspirational words of my daughter, "You have to try like a gorilla, not like a mouse, Mommy." I wish all of you the strength. If you look inside yourself, you will find it.

Until one is committed, there is hesitancy,
the chance to draw back,
always ineffectiveness.
Concerning all acts of initiative (and
creation), here is one elementary truth —
the ignorance of which kills countless
ideas and splendid plans:
that the moment one definitely commits
oneself, then Providence moves, too.
All sorts of things occur to help one
that would never otherwise have occurred.
A whole stream of events issues from the
decision, raising in one's favor
all manner of unforeseen incidents and
meetings and material assistance,
which no man could have dreamed
would have come his way.
Whatever you can do, or dream you can,
begin it.
Boldness has genius, power
and magic in it. Begin it now.

Goethe

Janet Gosch

Where to go for help and information

After meeting with many different counselors and therapists on a variety of issues after my divorce, the one common piece of advice they all gave me was, "Now you need to read and get more information so you can find ways to help yourself and your family."

Janet Gosch

Books, phone numbers and addresses which may prove helpful

The American Association of Marriage and Family Therapy
1133 15th St. N.W., Suite #300
Washington, D.C. 20005
(202) 452-0109

For Learning How to Cope With your Anger and Frustration

How to Collect Your Child Support by Julieanne Griffin
Adams Media — 1995
(781) 767-8100

Child Support Enforcement
(private child support "hunters of deadbeat dads")
800 801-KIDS

Association for Children for Enforcement of Support
(ACES)
2260 Upton Avenue
Toledo, OH 43606
800-537-7072 — For more information on a chapter near you

Children's Rights Council, Inc. (CRC)
300 Eye St. N.E., Suite #401
Washington, D.C. 20002 800-787-KIDS
(202) 547-6227
Lobbies nationally on behalf of parents as to the divorce
and support laws that affect them

Long-Distant Parenting by Miriam Galper Cohen
(Signet) **1989**
Out of print but check your local library for a copy

The Written Connection is a package of helpful material
for a non-custodial parent. It contains 12 months of
structured communication materials, providing for four
mailings per month, plus a guidebook. For kids-aged four
to 12. (Indicate your child's age)
Send $29.95 plus $4.00 postage to:
The Write Connection
P.O. Box 293
Lake Forest, CA 92630
         or
call 800-334-3143

Child Custody; Building Agreements That Work by
MimiLyster
(Nolo Press) **1995**
800-992-6656
Ideas for a win-win custody agreement

Joint Custody Association
10606 Wilkins Avenue
Los Angeles, CA
(310) 475-5352
An important resource for legislative information

**Families Apart: 10 Keys To Successful Shared
Parenting** by Melinda Blau
Perigree, **1993**

Healing Hearts
by Elizabeth Hickey and E. Dalton (Family Connections)
1994
(801) 484-2100
Includes financial worksheets and a parenting agreement

Marriage, Divorce and Nullity: A Guide to the Annulment Process in the Catholic Church
Liturgical Press
Collegeville, MN
800-858-5450

Office of Child Support Enforcement
U.S. Dept. of Health and Human Resources
901 D St. S.W.
Aerospace Center — 4 th Floor
Washington, D.C. 20447
(202) 401-9373
Information on how Uncle Sam can help you to collect your child support. This center also publishes a national newsletter and provides other informative booklets. For a free copy of their Handbook on Child Support Enforcement, call their National Reference Center at (202) 401-9383.

EXPOSE
P.O. Box 11191
Alexandria, VA 22312
(703) 941-5844
For military spouses in a divorce in need of referrals and information

HELP FOR CHILDREN IN THE CLASSROOM

Interaction Publishing
1825 Gillespie Way, Suite #101
El Cajon, CA 92020
800-359-0961
They publish a manual of a model program called Banana Splits: A Peer Support Program for the Survivors of Divorce Wars

RAINBOWS
2100 Golf Rd., Suite #370
Rolling Meadows, IL 60008
(847) 952-1770
Information on peer support groups for children and young adults held at sites in almost every state

PRESCHOOL-AGE BOOKS

Let's Talk About It: Divorce by Fred Rogers
Putnam, 1996
A photo essay book that talks about feelings during divorce in Mr. Rogers' wonderfully caring way
800-788-6262

Where is Daddy? The Story of a Divorce by Beth Goff
Beacon Press, 1969
A moving story about a little girl's confusion and fear of being abandoned when her parents divorce. Her parents fight, dad moves out, and mom goes to work.
(617) 742-2110

ELEMENTARY SCHOOL AGE BOOKS

The Divorce Workbook: A Guide for Kids and Families by Ives, Fassler & Lash
Waterfront Books
Burlington, VT 05401
1985
A workbook to help children sort out feelings and understand the "legal stuff"
800-639-6063

Why Are We Getting a Divorce? by Peter Mayle
Crown, 1978/1988
This book deals with difficult issues such as why people marry, divorce, misconceptions, living with one parent, and dealing with feelings
(212) 572-6117

PRE-TEEN AND TEENAGE BOOKS

How It Feels When Parents Divorce by Jill Krementz
Knopf, 1984
In this touching book, beautifully illustrated with the author's photographs, 20 girls and boys ages seven to 16 express their feelings about their parents' divorces
(212) 751-2600

It's Not the End of the World By Judy Blume
Dell, 1972
Judy Blume tackles the problem of divorce through the eyes of a 12 year old girl, a middle child of three.
800-223-5780

SUPPORT GROUPS AND OTHER RESOURCES

Parents Without Partners
401 N. Michigan Ave.
Chicago, IL 60611
800-637-7974
(312) 644-6610
Best known organized singles group with 1,200 local chapters in the United States and Canada. They offer discussion groups, workshops, children's programs and social events

Step Families
650 J St., Suite #205
Lincoln, NE 68508
(402) 477-7837
They sponsor chapters across the country

The Step Family Foundation
333 West End Ave.
New York, NY 10023
(212) 877-3244
They offer counseling seminars and a newsletter

American Bar Association Dispute Resolution Center
740 15th Street N. W. — 9th Floor
Washington, D.C. 20005
(202) 662-1690

Association of Family and Conciliation Courts
329 W. Wilson St.
Madison, WI 53703
(608) 251-4001

ADDRESSES ON THE COMPUTER

On-Line therapy directory referral service can be found on the Internet at: http://www.psychology.com/therapy

Children's Rights Council, Inc. (CRC)
www.vix.com/crc

The Administration for Children and Families
www.acf.dhhs.go

Single Rose Resource for Single Mothers
www.singlerose.com
P.O. Box 487
Kennedale, TX 76060

The Divorce Support Page
www.hughson.com

Divorce Helpline
www.divorcehelp.com

Divorce On-Line
www.divorce-online.com

Divorce Source
www.divorcesource.com

Step Family Association of America
www.stepfam.org

American Bar Association Dispute Resolution Center
www.abanet.org

Association of Family and Conciliation Courts
www.afcc@afccnet.org

Final Thoughts

We as Americans must realize how divorce is affecting our children, the children who are the future of this great country. With the high divorce rate in America, our children are not learning how to develop healthy relationships. They are not being given the chance to grow up with innocence, confidence and security.

America was built first and foremost on the strength of the family unit. For if there is a strong home base, the children learn, grow and are nutured in a positive atmosphere. When a child is raised in a divorce situation, they many times do not get the opportunity to learn how to function in a solid family unit of mother, father and children.

We have to stop jumping into marriage with the thought that if it doesn't work out, we'll just move on, especially when there are children involved.

We need to shape America's future to be confident and secure and America's future is our children.

Janet Gosch

Janet Gosch